DEDICATION

This work is primarily dedicated to my mother and father.
Their strength, courage and understanding have always been
the wall I had to lean on from childhood to manhood.
Everything I am is a direct result of their love and guidance.

For
Marvin Williamson Sr.
And
Zaheerah Sudan Rahman
(aka: Flora Mae Williamson)
[May They Rest In Peace]
I know their spirit will continue to touch us all
And contribute to the greatness in each of their descendants

*I was diagnosed with non small cell cancer in February 2012.
As a result, I decided to revisit a great deal of my past. This
book is a big part of that past. 17 years ago I dedicated this
book to my parents. I still dedicate this book to the man and
woman who played such an important part in who I am but I
would be remiss not to add my loving wife to that dedication.
She is, as she was then, the muse for every love driven piece of
work in this book. I love her just as much now as I did 17
years ago and the world needs to know what Carolyn
Williamson means to me. My wife and my parents are still
the ones responsible for who I am and, by the Grace of God,
who I may still yet become.*

COPYRIGHT 1995
RAW PUBLICATIONS
ISBN 978-0-9647809-0-9

LOVE

PRELUDE TO LOVE 4

I WANT YOU 5

IF I 5

GODS' GIFT 6

UNTITLED #1 6

JUST LOVING YOU 7

UNTITLED #2 7

FOR ME 8

WHO BUT YOU? 9

LAST NIGHT 9

TO BE CONTINUED 10

A LOVE SHARED 11

BLACK WOMAN 12

MY MOTHERS EYES 13

DIFFERENT 14

WHEN LOVE GETS OLD 15

JUST BECAUSE 16

LIKE A BLACK 17
WOMAN

ANGER

PRELUDE TO ANGER 19-23

GAS LEAK 24-25

—

2

MY ANGER MY RAGE	26-27
WHEN	28
I REMEMBER	29-30
TALK SENSE	31
LITTLE BLACK BABIES	32-33
FALSEHOOD	34-35
ODE TO MR. CHARLIE	36-37
CHILDREN OF THE NIGHT	38-40
BUT I DO LIKE WHITE POETS	41-43
THIS IS FOR MY NIGGAS'	44-45
WHEN THEY COME FOR US	46-47
DEMON FOR ALL SEASONS	48-49
WHAT IF?	50-51
A LETTER TO MY HERO	52-54
WHEN I CAME INTO THEIR LIVES, I DIDN'T KNOW	55-56
A NIGHT IN THE LIFE	57-58

PRELUDE TO LOVE

It's not so difficult to understand love, but the infinite lack of it in our world today, is beyond the scope of reasoning. It takes less effort to love thousands than it does to hate just one. But the Black man chooses hate over love, deceit over trust and apathy over understanding. We would rather eliminate each other than eliminate the shallow emotional and inherited barriers that keep us from living as one.

Love is vital to our future. If the Black man is to continue to exist, he must learn to love; to love his self, to love his mate, to love his family and to love life.

Man did not earn the right to live. Through the love of God, he was given that right. We must learn to love God by loving his creations, (ourselves), or truly forfeit that right to live.

✳✳✳

I WANT YOU

I want you.
I want you soft
As soft as your breath against my flesh
I want you warm
As warm as a welcome from two sets of lips
I want you wet
Not damp with sweat
But flowing
'till the energy, the passion, the pleasure
and the joy are one
I want you spent
I want you

IF I

If I could conjure a dream
From beginning to end
If I could plan my life
From here to eternity
If I could fashion my mate
To suit my needs
And if I could control the thoughts and moods of
others...
..........................Then I wouldn't need you

GODS' GIFT

Gods' greatest gift to man
Is woman
A major miracle
Of all that's beautiful and blessed

Love, respect and adoration
Are her god given rights
Pleasure, moral support
And infinite enthusiasm
Are her god given talents

Any man
Who assumes he has the right
Or the ability
To change who she is
Or hinder her existence
Is committing a hazardous sin

UNTITLED #1

Separate wills
Do not jeopardize a loving relationship.
But separate ideals
In regards to what love is
will
In order for such a relationship to exist
You must learn to live together as individuals
But you must also learn to love as one

JUST LOVING YOU

From dawn until dawn again
In joy that will never end
As wishes and dreams come true
In love with just loving you

I look, and I realize
My heart's beating in your eyes
God's blessed everything we do
In love with just loving you

A prayer floats across my mind
That we'll stay as one in time
And here's something you already knew
I'm in love with just loving you

UNTITLED #2

I'm too much of a man
To shout it out loud
So I'll just keep my joy to myself

Maybe if I close my eyes
You won't see the pleasure I feel
Or the feelings I pleasure

If you could see what loving you does to me
As you and passion play with my mind
You might think less of me.

FOR ME

I felt saddened
More often than not
Rather mad
But you were there for me

I felt hurt
Unnecessary
And no longer needed
But you were there for me

I showed signs
Of a self inflicted
Insanity
And you were there for me

Now I feel loved
Happy with my life
And at peace with myself
Because
You'll be there for me

WHO BUT YOU?

Who has the better vantage?
Who can see you as you truly are?
Your innermost wants and needs
Are open only to God and yourself...
.......until you love someone.

LAST NIGHT

Last night
I dreamed that we made love
A love so deep and intense
That our bodies trembled
A love so soaked with passion
That pleasure floated from within
Like heated waves against the shores
Of our very being
Joy crept up my spine
And into my mind
On tiny fingers of frantic sensitivity

The need to satisfy
And the need to be satisfied did battle
And both won

I awoke to find you watching me
With a drained look
And a content smile

You gently kissed my lips and said
"Last night I dreamed that we made love
A love so deep and intense........"

TO BE CONTINUED

Over and over I've told myself
And over and over I've listened

Every reason I can give myself
For loving you
Gives birth
To every reason there is
For loving you

Everything I feel
Reinforces
The way I feel.

Every thought of you
Is simply a continuation
Of a prior thought of you.

There is no cycle
For a cycle,
Sooner or later,
Returns to its' beginning.

I feel that our love
By God was planned
And in a sense,
Has always been

Therefore,
Where there was no beginning
There can be no end.
It can only continue...and grow.

■■

——

A LOVE SHARED

A love shared
Is two souls bared to each other.
Dropping the masquerade
And letting the truth breathe freely

A love shared
Is me feeling your pain
And you feeling my need
As we comfort each other

A love shared
Is me looking into your eyes
And realizing the sorrows of our past
And the joys our present union has brought us

A love shared
Is feeling your presence in my minds touch
Seeing your face in my minds eye
Knowing that no distance put between us
Could actually separate us

A love shared
Is an almost mystic bond
That keeps us feeling as one.
With the heart of a Siamese twin
Forever a life giving part of each other

A love shared
Is what we have and what we will have
Always.

BLACK WOMAN

Black woman
Regal in your different shades
And hues
Mother of mine
Daughter of mine
Sister of mine

Mine
Mine to protect
And respect
Not to neglect
Or resurrect

Black woman
Cherished for your mythical ways
And moods
Passion of mine
Lover of mine
Lust of mine

Mine
Mine to hold
And behold
Not to control
Or remold

Mine

MY MOTHER'S EYES

When I look into my mother's eyes
I see dreams fulfilled
And dreams let go
I see pride in her being
And in all the things she knows

I see hope that there will be time
To do all the things she must
I see prayers spoken for her children
And I see her faith in all of us

I see struggles started
On our behalf
And hurt in those eyes
Even when they laugh

I see hard lessons learned
And all the pain they wrought
I see a life of sacrifices
 and the things for me they bought

I see my obligation
To make her life worthwhile
To do things in her honor
Because I am her child

DIFFERENT
(Ode To a Wedding Day)

At the end of this day
I will be different

Not a physical difference
That the eyes can see,
But a difference you'll notice
Just the same

My smile will be different,
My laugh will be different,
And the beat of my heart
Will be different

At the end of this day
My world will be different,
Not quite the rapture
But different just the same.

The sun will shine as I smile,
A breeze will blow as I laugh,
And the earth will turn
With the beat of my heart.

At the end of this day
I will be your other half,
And god has already promised,
That when tomorrow comes
I will still be loved,
And the rest of my life will be
Different

WHEN LOVE GETS OLD

When dust gathers where it shouldn't
And dirt congeals in freshly opened wounds
Seeds of hurt and betrayal take root

When what was sweet and slightly different
Becomes bitter and common
Apathy makes its presence known

When passion is remembered
But no longer felt
Each memory becomes a bearer of great pain

When love gets old
So does the heart
And the soul,
And both will die...

...If I don't walk away

JUST BECAUSE

Just because love hurts now
Doesn't mean it will hurt forever
And it doesn't mean I'll avoid it
From now on

Just because love hurts now
Doesn't mean that I don't need it
And it doesn't mean that I won't seek it soon

Because love hurts now
 Means I must be careful
When I again choose to give
My heart

Because love hurts now
Means that next time there will be
More reservations
More doubt
And less trust

And the one I pass
May be the one I shouldn't

LIKE A BLACK WOMAN

I want every Black Woman
Not because I'm conceited enough
to think I'm the greatest lover
but because I know every Black Woman is

No woman can make love
like A Black Woman
No mind and/or body
responds
In the throes of passion
Like A Black Woman's

No woman
can make A man
cry, scream, shake, rock, wrestle
sweat, pray, even pay, beg, plead
(Please baby, baby please)
feel the need
toss that seed
(Whew!)
Like A Black Woman

PRELUDE TO ANGER

Throughout the history of so-called modern man, the Black race has always suffered the brunt of oppression, persecution and outright hatred. There has been a policy that has been subliminally inbred, generation after generation, that has other races convinced that we are at the root of this countries woes, and in many cases, the woes of this world in general. There is a seemingly eternal attitude that says, "The world would be so much better if we just eliminate the Black race." Thus we as a people have found ourselves under constant attack and ridicule.

It is my hope that my people understand the not so hidden implications of the November '94' elections and the resulting cuts in programs of all kinds that directly effect, or are intended to directly effect, us. With the trend of the 90s' already leaning toward black conservatism, which in my mind is tantamount to treason, and the uprooting of the democratic and black foothold (not stronghold) over Washington, our State has taken a dramatic turn for the worse. Many, like myself, had become complacent and trusting. Knowing those in charge, for the devious individuals they are, did not stop me from once again believing that there were signs of positive change in the air.

Don't get me wrong, a democrat or an independent is still a politician and the American political system is designed for both the crooked and the soon to be crooked, so there's no love lost on either. What concerns me is that with the House, the Senate and almost seventy-five percent of the country under republican rule, the need to be discreet with the kicks in the head that Black folks are about to receive, are non-existent.

Every program and government policy that is being changed or has been threatened to change, directly effects the black race without any regard to class or position. We have everything to lose and nothing to gain by sitting idly by.

Around the same time as the beginning of the civil rights movement, a concerted effort was initiated to destroy the credibility and the humanity of the black race. The primary tools used in this effort have been lies, deceit and manipulation. Through the ingenious use of these tools, those in charge have not only succeeded in making the rest of the world terrified at the sight or thought of us, but have also succeeded in making too many of us fear and loathe ourselves.

Somehow we must realize, and make our children realize, that we have been manipulated by the best. Their ultimate goal becomes more obvious every day. By manipulating our thinking and reactions, they will get us to the point where they can do anything that they deem necessary to keep us in line, and be able to justify it in the eyes of all those concerned, including our own people.

If we are to survive as a race of strong, black and beautiful people, then every one of us who knows about or remembers the struggles, the gains and the losses our people have suffered through, must share that knowledge. There is an old saying that states, "The only dumb question is the one not asked." Through the sharing of "knowledge of self" we can again stimulate the minds of our young and old and make them not only ask the questions but demand the answers.

The things we have been through as a people, must be remembered, but we cannot dwell on them. The trials and tribulations that we as a people have been forced to suffer must be understood, but again, we cannot dwell on them. Through it all we have survived. The reason that we have been able to survive, even though the odds were insanely against it, is that we have always found strength in our families and we could always find our true selves in our community.

When we were first captured and brought to this country as slaves, one of the first things that was done was the destruction of any family unit. We survived by turning to our newfound community and establishing and re-establishing new family units. Family and community have always been and will always be inseparable. The simple fact that our families and our community are always shown in a negative light should show you that even those who would see us destroyed and eliminated know where our strengths lie.

Today I feel that we have reached a turning point in our existence. Regardless of outside attitudes and influence, we as a people must now reestablish and strengthen our family and community or be prepared to perish from the face of this earth. We no longer have the luxury of waiting to have our independence handed to us or waiting for someone else to fight for it on our behalf.

We are at war and a long standing and successful tactic of any war has been the "divide and conquer" tactic. Through planning and conditioning, we have been divided.

The emasculation of the black male has contributed greatly to this division. The emasculated son of an emasculated father cannot function as needed in a family unit. Even the undying strength that has made the black woman the survivor she is has been used to divide the black family. She, like the black male, has been convinced that one does not need the other to survive. Yes it is true that they can survive as an individual but neither is complete or will survive as a whole, without the other. This attitude that we have acquired is not of our own choosing, even though we have been convinced that it is. In kind, we have instilled this destructive attitude in our young and we are now beginning to pay the price. Our children have lost all respect for themselves and their race. Which means that they cannot hold any esteem for anything or anyone that is directly connected to their past or present. At the top of this list is family and community.

A lot of what I'm saying has been rehashed over and over again, but repetition means nothing. As I said before, we as a people have reached a turning point. We have been divided but not conquered. Our lives and our lifestyles have been attacked and now it is time for us to mount an all out counter attack.

There are potentially great men and women in those angry misguided youth out there in the streets. We must re-establish the family ethic and family unity and bring those lost and angry youths back into the fold. We must turn to the hero in all of us and save ourselves, "by any means necessary." In the each of us there is an inherent good. In each of us, regardless of career choice or choice of lifestyle, there is a multitude of wisdom. It will take combined effort of every black man, woman and child to knock down the walls of destructive pride, ego and indifference and re-establish the love, courage and invincibility that the black family represents. Once we set the wheels in motion to accomplish this, the natural by-product will be a strong unified community of black people who not only know who they are, but also know what they are and what they can and shall be. We see the results of random acts of violence against ourselves every day. Each black individual should commit him or herself to one random act of blackness daily. Positive acts that will endlessly breed positive results. Acts that will inevitably strengthen our people by strengthening our community. We cannot alienate ourselves from ourselves and survive.

When you see a child speaking wrongly of himself or his race, correct that child intelligently, not with ridicule or arrogance. If you see a man, woman or child, being eaten alive by drugs, go to them with love and understanding. Do whatever it takes to bring them back into the fold. We cannot allow the things one has or does not have, to take away from the fact that they are each a valuable member of our race.

Every black man needs his black woman. Every black woman needs her black man. Every black child needs his black mother and father. Even if, for whatever reasons, they do not see eye to eye enough to stay together as a couple, they must at least realize that the child must be able to turn to each parent individually and receive a common message. That message being that even a displaced family is still a family bound by blood and honor and that any family is the breeding seed for a strong community.   The bottom line is this. A family is a mini- community. A community is an extended family. One cannot and will not survive without the other.

The future of the black family, the black community and, indeed, the black race, depends on the willingness of each black individual to commit that random act of blackness and insure that we as a people will survive.

Each One Teach One

GAS LEAK ON THE THIRD TIER

Like a caged beast
That's caught the predators scent
I strain my brain
As I take a deeper whiff

Paced the catwalk
Roamed the dayroom
And the odor saturating my nerves
Is stronger

Imagination?

Bruised my hands
Against the grey steel walls
I know the keeper hears me
But does he heed my call?

Panic
    Turns to
        Panic/Anger
As grown men try to hide their fear
In their egos'

Outer doors swing open
Three keepers saunter in
Smiles clash with the
Angry........Pleading.......Whimpers

They don't smell a thing
Can't smell a thing
Won't smell a thing
Until we're re-locked in

The smiles...
          ...Again a grin
A joke within
Here's the problem
Unplug the T.V.!

Is this how/where we'll die?
Caged
Abandoned animals
That no one called for in time?

......Gas 'em!

Victims of an accident/joke

The keepers leave
There's no reprieve
Their laughter chokes us
Like the fumes that permeate
This domicile of the doomed

Grown fears...Grown tears
Cries for Mama...Cries for God
Cries for life

Kiss the floor
Does gas rise?
Bury my face in the piss-stained toilet
Putrid lives follow putrid water
Down the drain

Is this how/where we'll die?
Some innocent...some guilty
Some guilty of being innocent
Is this how/where we'll die?

MY ANGER MY RAGE

Even as a child
As the angry clouds encroached
Upon the ever darkening sky
As the wind pushed
        And pulled
And stirred the waste from the gutters
Of the city streets
As the lightning flashed
Eliminating normal shadows
Wwhile creating newer and stranger ones

And

The ever growing sound of thunder
Told the tale of that to come
As the chill of the first drops of rain
Upon my face
Awoke memories that were not my own
        I felt the storm within

Even in my youth
In the night-like day
        When the storms
Showed their energy
Like a badge of courage
Snatching up history by its' roots
Crushing it into splinters
In its' eternal grip
Flinging it and myself to the ground
Daring us to stand and grow again
        I felt the storm rage
Even to this day

As the anger swells
And threatens to overflow the horizon
And conflict and confusion
Struggle at the seams of existence
Until self-destruction
Seems the only escape......
As the clouds burst
A storm of my own rage
Rages within

WHEN

When White People trip
Why do my People take the fall?

When these oafs and ogres
Slip in the indignation
Of their own shit,
Why must my People suffer the stench?

When evil is caught
By the evil it does,
Why must my people be the blood stained alibis'?

When tears are shed
As the rights of human beings
Are violated elsewhere,
Does my peoples violation
Relieve your guilt?

When all is said and done,
When God calls in all debts,
Will my People pay the bill,
Or will they cash the check?

I REMEMBER A TIME
(AKA:A RACE DIVIDED
CAN'T STAND ITSELF)

I remember a time
When we just wanted to be
When we just wanted to be Black

I remember a time
When we didn't want to be, couldn't want to be
Black Muslims
We just wanted to be Black

I remember a time
When we didn't want to be
Couldn't want to be
Black Panthers
We just wanted to be Black

I remember a time
When we didn't want to be
Couldn't let ourselves be
Negroes or Coloreds or Afro-Americans
Or NAACP'ers or SNCC'ers or YAWF'ers or
Baptist or Episcopalians or Jehovahs' Witnesses
Or Democrats or Republicans or
Conservative or Liberal or Old Niggers or New Niggers
Or House Niggers or any Niggers

I remember a time
When we came together
And White Folks got scared
"We got ta do sumpthin' Capn' Cotchipee!
Our Niggers done lost they mind!"

........And they pacified us
And we forgot what we
Didn't want to be
Couldn't want to be
Shouldn't want to be
Until that time faded from our memory

And now,
We're just, Preachers and Followers and Lookers
And Losers and Lifers and Niggers and Niggers
And.........

TALK SENSE

What sense does it make
Tget angry and then close your eyes
To what made you angry?
What sense does it make
To demand justice and not be willing
To fight for it?
What sense does it make
To de-educate yourself
With hard drugs
Hard liquor
And hard bull
And at the same time
Speak of a desperate need for a revolution?
What sense does it make
To scream of Black pride
When all you're really proud of
Is your last hustle
And the green of the money
It got you?

Don't speak to me
Of Black pain if you've never felt it.
Don't speak to me
Of Black History if you've never lived it.
Don't speak to me
Of Black pride if you've never had it.
Most of all
Don't speak to me
Until you can get mad and stay mad,
Until you can demand justice and go get it,
Until you can re-educate yourself
And start a revolution,
Until you can talk with good sense,
Don't talk to me!

LITTLE BLACK BABIES

I love little Black Babies
And the women who bear them

I love their little Black eyes
As they recognize
A familiar face
A familiar place
And those eyes flow
Into that little Black smile that I love

I love their little Black lips
And their little Black voices
That go goo and ga and gurgle

I love their little Black laughs
And their little Black gasps
Of anticipation
As their little Black arms
And their little Black legs
Pump furiously at feeding time
When the nipple nears
Or their attention is peaked
By their little Black wants

I love their little Black hands
That grip with imagined strength
And poke and probe
Every new found discovery
I love their little Black feet
And their little Black toes
That push and wiggle
In preparation for the time
They'll make that first stand

I love those little Black Babies
Who are future Black Men
And future Black Women

And God knows
I would kill for
And die for
Those little Black Babies
And the Women who bear them

FALSEHOOD

I can't see the distant shore
The miles and mist obscure my view
Occasional
Glimpses of the horizon reveal nothing

Standing here with my back to reality
My feet planted firmly
On the brink of shattered faith

I am confused

The roiling glass before me
Seduces me calmly
While the truth beats at my back

The oceans width and depth
Exudes serenity
While the truth wraps it's breath
Coldly around my neck
Like a bitter omen
God's world lies before me
All natural in its beauty and mystery

At its' wildest moments
It is still his
Even when his clouds shield the horizon
I know his Sun is out there
I know that what is below
He placed in those depths

I would rather spend my life
Admiring his work

To be a part of this shore
On an eternal watch
Would be a blessing

But the truth erodes this fantasy
And I cannot turn my back
On the horrors born of mans' inequities

Sooner or later
I must turn and face the truths behind me

For God did not say,
"Lay down and feel safe in your beliefs in me."
He wants us to fight
For his right
His truth

Hell is This world of contradictions

The truth that we struggle with everyday
Is neither His will or His way

NOW THAT THE REVOLUTION HAS STARTED
(AKA: ODE TO MR. CHARLIE)
(AKA: OWED TO MR. CHARLIE)

Once Mr. Charlie had himself a mule.
Mr. Charlie said that it was good and true.
No matter how bad he beat it,
Or how often he didn't feed it,
The mule still did what it was told to do.

One day as Mr. Charlie beat that mule.
The mule felt it was time to change the rules.
So Mr. Charlie shot it, and later thought about it,
And wondered, "What got into that damned mule?"

So foolish Charlie bought himself a dog.
A vicious, full of bloodlust kind of dog.
And often he would beat it,
Gunpowder he would feed it,
So it would well protect his happy home.

Then one day when Old Charlie kicked that pup.
It turned on him and damned near ate him up.
He couldn't understand it,
"That dog! How underhanded!"
And calmly shoved a knife into it's gut.

Then dumb ass Charlie bought himself a boat!
Filled with my people it could hardly float!
For years he did enslave us,
Deceive us and betray us,
And swore it was our destiny he wrote!

Now I don't know why some can't understand!

———

If animals can turn then so will Man!
How can you just abuse me,
Find pride in how you use me,
And think I won't cut your throat when I can!?
If fucked up Charlie had been blessed with brains!
He'd know the shit he pulled was just insane!
But since it hasn't reached you,
You can't abuse Gods' creatures,
And not expect a few lumps in return!

And now that we've decided to fight back!
You say that we don't know how we should act!
But since you were our teacher,
Throughout this horror feature,
I think we're acting right! Aint that a fact?!

CHILDREN OF THE NIGHT

Children of the night,
Sleeping through the wisdom.
Minds as empty
As the fortys' they toss away

Victims of design,
Designer clothes,
Designer drugs,
Designer suicide
By designer guns,
Designer Genocide,
By design.

Children of the night.
Too tired to rise with the sun.
Tired eyes,
Tired ears,
Damaged windows and doorways
To a mind too numb
To hear or see the truth

Jammin'
Go on, play it louder.
Your favorite song
You know the one,
That Hoe, Bitch, Nigger Song.
Play it louder!
Play that beat
Until you beat into your mind
What they couldn't beat
Into your Ancestors mind.
Until you yourself believe

That that's all you ever were
(HOE)
All you'll ever see
(BITCH)
All that you can be
(NIGGER)

No time for the true lesson
Too busy soakin' in the new lesson
Hate Thyself!
      Fool Thyself!
            Kill Thyself!
Self taught? I don't think so.

Children of the night
Schooled by the new rules
Your heroes are zeroes
Much like yourself
Can't earn
Can't learn
Can't see a future
Can't have a past.
White Man said it,
Must be true,
So do what you gotta do.
Buy the White Mans' dope
Sell it to your own.
Who says the customers'
Got to be grown.
Buy the White Mans' guns
And the White Mans' bullets
And kill those Black Babies
And Black Mothers
And Black Fathers
And yo' Black self
For dissin' yo' self!

Children of the night
Please see the light
To convince us there's no hope
Is his only hope.
Get Back to Blackness
Before there's no Blackness
To get back to.
■■

BUT I DO LIKE WHITE POETS!

What's that you say?
Why do I read so much?
Why do I read so much Poetry?
Why do I read so much Black Poetry?

What's wrong?
Black folks aint supposed to read?

I've read White Poets.
I was taught Poetry
With White egg-zamples.

If I want to read
About eyes like lakes,
I read White Poets.

If I want to read
About hair like spun gold,
I read White Poets.

If I want to read
About this Gory/Glorified Country
I read White Poets.

But your rhymes are not mine
They do not express
Me.

So.
If I want to read
About my fears,
I read Black Poets.

If I want to read
About my pain,
I read Black Poets.
What?
What's that you say?
Everything I read is negative?

Maybe you didn't hear me.

If I want to read
About your interpretation
Of a peaceful Summers' Eve
I'll read White Poets.

If I want to read
About the strength of the mighty Oak,
I'll read White Poets.

But you made the world Black and White,
And you made the negative.
God didn't intend for the complexion
To be complex.

Unlike the negative
Of a Black and White photo,
Where White becomes Black,
Black becomes White,
My negative is not yours
And yours could never
Become mine.

My Summer Eves'
Are not peaceful,
So I read Black Poets.

I find my strength

In my Peoples words,
So I read Black Poets.

I could stop reading.
I could stop reading and react.
I could stop reading and react negatively.

But I'll just sit here,
For now,
And read Black Poets.

THIS IS FOR MY NIGGAS?

Teen scene
Young men standin' round the boom box
Rappin'
Talkin' crappin'
Bass beat
Vibratin' the concrete

What's the 411
With these
Men/Children?

Seemin' happy
Bouncin'
Laughin'
Hand slappin'
Pants hangin'
3 of a kind
1 Black
1 White
1 Black and White
All young

No worry
No hurry
Life is a day to day
Get away

Here comes another
Young and full of
Wonder what's on his mind?

Seemin' happy

Bouncin'
Laughin'
Hands slappin'

White hand
Slaps Black hand
White
Man/Child says,
"Here's my Nigga!"

Black Men/Children
Didn't miss a beat
Maybe he'll repeat

But will they understand?

WHEN THEY COME FOR US

When they come for us
Will they catch you nappin'?
Will they rock you to sleep
In your sleep?

Will they win the war
Of wills
Of minds
Of ethnicity
Without breaking a sweat?

When they come for us
Will they find you wrapped
In 40's dreams and crack-caine wishes
Waiting for a miracle from a God
You don't believe in anyway?

Will you be too Right-Wing
To be Right Black?
Or too much a light thing
To be Right Black?

When they come for us
Will they find you on your knees
Begging for mercy
From a merciless host
Offering phallic pleasures
In exchange for your life?

Or when they come for us
Will they find that they were expected?
Will they find the doors to our existence
Locked and defended?

Will they find
An impassible wall
Of Black Men, Women and Children
Armed with the intelligence
Of generation after generation
Of proud Black Kings and Queens
And Revolutionaries?

When they come for us
Expecting submission,
Expecting us to roll over
And give up the Ghost

Will we be ready??

DEMON FOR ALL SEASONS

The Winter is his cold hard truth
As evil lies dormant
Beneath a blanket of white lies

Stagnant lives
Shatter in the wind
Like lifeless, Ic covered, Brittle Branches

This is his Season

The Spring
Is his time of false hope
As new life
Struggles toward the Sun

Children
Like newborn blades of grass
Find little resistance
And wonder if
Now is their time
But this too is his Season

The Summer is his harshest joke
When Evil imitates hibernation
And allows it's minions
And adversaries
To taste freedom

Creatures and colors
Misrepresent our state
As warmth and beauty
Blinds us to our fate

For this is also his Season

And then comes Fall
And Evil has elected to be elected
As the cycle ends

Making a mockery
Of the Son of hope
As he wishes
You would very merrily kiss his freshly wiped ass!

The Demon owns all Seasons

WHAT IF?

What would this country be called
If my ancestors had joined forces
With the likes of Geronimo,
With the Commanche or the Seminole?

What sort of people would rule this land
If we had joined each other
Instead of trying to impress
The oppressor
With our willingness to be loyal
If only we would be accepted?
Would the rivers run cleaner?
Could the air be justly called
Fresh?

What sort of laws
Would there be to enforce
If we had joined forces
With Sitting Bull or Zapata?

What colors would Old Glory be?
Would our Blues bleed Red
Without the White?

Would there have been a need
For a Custer
A Hitler
A McCarthy
A Lenin
A Jim Jones
............A King?

What if people of color
Had found themselves unique?

———

Would they have trusted as they did?
Would they have welcomed as they did?

What if people of color
Had stopped the lies and manipulation
Where it started
And drove the White Plague
Back to the shores that gave it birth?

Would Europe be America?
Poisoned by its' own?
Raped by its' own?
Would Europe be America the miracle
Surviving its' own evil?

What if we had joined
Our Brothers in South Africa
Or if they had joined us?
But they too had been manipulated
Into seeing us as less

Less than proud
Less than able
Less than Black
Less than Human
Less than less

Like every immigrant
Past and present
Who has gained acceptance
By not accepting us

From Shaka to Castro
No one has ever wondered...
What if?

A LETTER TO MY HERO

Dear Hero:

I'm sorry. I don't remember your name or what you looked like. I think I was only 15 or 16 at the time and i had juvenile things on my mind. There's a lot about you that I don't remember and I regret it. What you did deserves to be remembered and honored. I do remember the basic facts. I think it was in St. Louis and I know it was a Howard Johnsons' hotel where you made your mark in history.

When I first noticed that what was on the T.V. screen was a news bulletin, my first thought was, "I'd rather be watching something else." There was a high angle camera shot of the hotel and the street below. Several emergency vehicles were crowded in front of the building. A ladder from one of the fire trucks was extended to, what looked like, the 20th floor at least. Smoke was still pouring out of one window.

The announcer was saying that the firemen had responded to what was supposedly a normal call to a high rise structure fire, but when they arrived, they were met with automatic weapons fire from one of the upper floors of the hotel. Police were called and the streets surrounding the building were sealed off. If I remember right, some of the firemen were hit.

The hotel was evacuated room by room, which took quite a while. The swat team was called and snipers were placed on nearby rooftops. The news people were in everybody's face and of course everybody had an opinion as to what was happening. "It was Russian terrorists." "It was left wing fanatics." "It was Black militants."

Throughout the day, shots were exchanged between the police and whoever had seized the hotel. The police reported that, based on the evidence they had so far, there had to be several armed individuals throughout the building. At one point, they thought that some of them had entered the heating and cooling system and were moving from spot to spot through the network of vent pipes and ducts.

As time passed, the law became frustrated because they had not seized the perpetrators, in spite of their Herculean efforts. A sudden volley of shots made them think that they had finally cornered their foes. However, radio communications soon told them that they were shooting each other, which I found hilarious.

After dark they found you and of course, killed you. They had to. You got the attention of the entire nation via television, and you made those highly trained law enforcement officials look like idiots. The ass kicker was that you did it all by yourself.

Of course, once they I.D.'d you, they had to make you seem insane. They played up the fact that you were a Vietnam vet and they slipped in the idea of after effects of such a traumatic experience, such as flashbacks. Also they had to throw in the suggestion of drug involvement. In other words, they had to show the public that insanity, natural or self induced, made you do what you did. Indeed I myself couldn't see a sane man taking on such a suicide mission. Shooting firemen didn't seem to make much sense either. I thought that since, in those days, anything in uniform and anything white represented carte blanche abuse to us that you just decided not to discriminate.

When they went to your apartment, they found all kinds of so-called militant rabble-rousing propaganda. They also found a note that made me realize that you were not insane. Not at all. In fact you were a hero. Black people were catching hell in those days. Catching hell for resisting the abuse we have suffered from our first days on these shores until the present. I don't know how many Black people were watching that day. Maybe it wasn't very many. Maybe, like myself, they couldn't see the importance of what you had done. I don't remember the entire message, like I said, it was a long time ago. I do remember one sentence though, one phrase that stuck in my mind for over 25 years. In your note you said, "I just wanted to show the world what one angry black man could do."

I wish more of us had heard you. I wish more of us had listened. I hope more of us remember.

Thank you

WHEN I CAME INTO
THEIR LIVES,
I DIDN'T KNOW.

When the bullet struck, the gates to Hell opened and he welcomed me. He explained how Gods' chosen he also chose, just to spite God. Then he thanked me for helping him destroy Gods' chosen. He thanked me for selling his drugs to the young and old and putting them to sleep. He thanked me for closing their hearts to emotion and their minds to reason.

I couldn't speak.

He thanked me for feeding his poison to the young mother whose unborn was destined to be another Doctor King.

And still I couldn't speak.

He thanked me for putting the gun in the hand of the man/child who worked for me. His stray bullet took the life of a young woman whose future medical knowledge would have saved thousands.

He said that was one of my best works
And I wished that I could speak.

He thanked me for taking the young toddler for collateral, leaving him with my fiend friends. While the mother went to work off her debt, they went to work on her son. Soon, he too would belong to Satan.

Then he smiled a smile drenched in evil and said, "I could have saved you from that bullet, but I don't do that, besides, you've already been replaced by more than a dozen willing souls. At this very moment, that girl that you refused credit to this morning is plunging a knife into her mother for the thirteenth time. I just love the number thirteen. Don't you? Anyway, later today she'll take her own life when she's realized what she's done. That idiot who shot you was her father. The police have him surrounded now, too stupid to know that his soul is already mine.

You people seem to forget that the thought of sin is also a sin so I'll end up with the souls of a few of those officers before the night is done. You see, deep down, they know who are the chosen and they don't like it any more than I do. But I digress. Several of the souls I'll receive today are the result of your work, and I just wanted to thank you."

I cried,
But I couldn't speak .

A NIGHT IN THE LIFE

Every night I think and remind myself of the fact, that as a Black man I am unique. I have unique experiences, unique wants and unique dreams. I also have unique fears, strengths and weaknesses. Nothing about me is irrational but too much about me is decided by others.

I could sit here and say that nothing effects me because I'm a strong-willed individual, but that would be a lie. I am a strong willed individual. I was beaten and driven into being that strong willed individual. Racism, treachery, oppression and hate are the tools YOU used to beat and drive me into being a STRONG-WILLED BLACK MAN. Even while you sit in your stolen homes on your stolen land with your stolen knowledge and tell me that all of this is my imagination or the result of searching for an excuse to fail, your arrogance makes me stronger.

Every night I think of and try to understand the mentality that makes you feel justified in your atrocities. What brain functions misfire or become corrupted and allow YOU to call yourself an emancipator or the guiding force of true democracy. You who are responsible for the destruction of civilization after civilization. You who are responsible for a multitude of genocidal tactics and techniques hidden in politics and policy. YOU whose duplicity gave form to the definition of "The Forked Toungue."

Every night I come to the realization that you have all the traits of the creature I swore was fictional when I was a young and foolish adolescent. As a Master manipulator you had me fooled, but I know too well now that the Devil does exist.

Every night I toss and turn in fitful sleep. Reliving the hell you put my ancestors through, the hell you've put me through and the hell you have planned for my children. BUT!!

Every morning I awake refreshed and calm. Half the battle of any war is knowing your enemy. I know you. I know you better than you know yourself. You see, I've discovered your weakness. In all of your attempts to destroy my past, present and future, YOU became arrogant. In your arrogance you have allowed yourself the undue luxury of believing you've won.

Everything in me that you think you've broken and destroyed, your arrogance has made stronger. Every part of me that you think you have manipulated and molded, has turned to dust in your hands. Those grains, swept by the unforgiving winds of true knowledge, will strip you of your false face of security...

....and one night you will lay down thinking that you've beaten me but you will wake up and realize that I've just begun to fight.